RULE #1
DON'T
BE #2

RULE

#1

DON'T BE #2

you get what you work for—
not what you wish for

Daniel Milstein

•

Library of Congress Control Number: 2017936004

ISBN 978-1-947165-03-8 (hardcover)
ISBN 978-1-947165-05-2 (ebook)

Visit our website at
DanMilstein.com
for more information.

Text design by Pauline Neuwirth, Neuwirth & Associates, Inc.
Original artwork by Katharine Schlansker
Edited by Pamela Gossiaux and Cheryl Baringer

Gold Star
PUBLISHING
A DIVISION OF THE GOLD STAR FAMILY OF COMPANIES

Dedicated to my wife Kelly.

You're not rich until you have something money can't buy.

Thank you for being you.

contents

SECTION ONE

Time to Pay the Rent

1

SECTION TWO

The Rules of Business Success

15

Make Hard Work Your Weapon

17

Go Big or Go Home

23

Keep Your Eyes on the Prize

31

Stand Up and Be Counted

39

Raise the Bar, Then Jump Over

47

Do It Now

55

Go All Out

63

Chart Your Course

69

Be Bold: Make the First Move

77

It's a Team Sport

85

Dreams Don't Work Unless You Do

93

Who Said It Would Be Easy?

101

Fake It Until You Make It

109

Get Real

117

Love the One You're With

125

An Overnight Success Usually Takes Ten Years

133

Get Off the Couch

141

Adapt and Conquer

149

You Can't Stop Believing

157

There's No Room for Complainers

165

Keep Your Enemies Close

173

Everyone Is Afraid of Something

183

Failure Is the Best Teacher

191

Always Be Closing

199

The World Is Full of Survivors

207

SECTION THREE

Turn Your Ideas Into Action

213

Rising to #1:

Never Give In. Never Give Up.

225

Acknowledgments

233

About the Author

235

section

1

Time to Pay the Rent

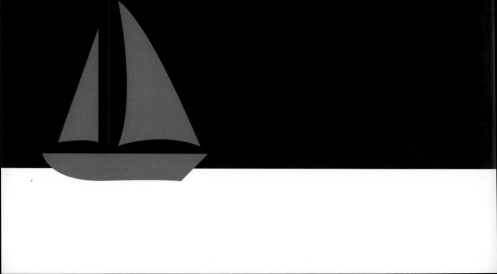

TIME TO PAY THE RENT

You can never cross the ocean unless you have the courage to lose sight of the shore.

●

Success. Everybody has an idea of what it means. Most people want it. But it's elusive. Many of the most intelligent and gifted people you know never achieve what we would consider success. Something is missing. Something's in their way.

By the time they have a solid "career," ninety-seven percent of the people who have a dream will have "settled" into a life of the mundane. Only three percent of those who dreamed of pursuing their passion will be successful. What's different about this three percent? I can tell you they weren't born with silver spoons, and they weren't simply luckier than the rest.

My own rocky road to lasting success has been both challenging and rewarding.

I was just 16-years-old when our plane landed in Detroit from the Soviet Union. The year was 1991 and we were fleeing from religious and political persecution. With 17 cents in my pocket and donated, second-hand clothes on my back, my biggest concern was surviving high school while learning to speak English. I had no idea where to begin.

But I was fortunate to get a job at McDonald's and sandwiched high school in between eight-hour shifts. The days were brutally long, but I was thrilled to have a job, and it taught me a work ethic that still serves me well. Today I'm one of the top residential financiers in the world, a sports and celebrity manager, movie producer, and best-selling author. I'm in the three percent.

I want you to be a success too. Here's why:

Knowing what I know, it's very frustrating—often heartbreaking—to watch people give up. But that's exactly what I witness, time and again, as I meet thousands of people at conferences, hockey rinks, and movie sets around the world. Most of them dream of being successful doing something they love. They want to be someone, achieve something, start over, or just begin. As we talk, they become excited about the opportunities they can see on their horizon, viewed from their "new" outlook. Then I see them again, a month, a year, or many years later, and they haven't moved. They're still on the couch, stuck in the dead-end job, relentlessly toiling away at a career they hate because somebody told them their dream is impractical—or worse, that *they* aren't good enough—and they stupidly believed what they'd heard. Or perhaps they failed and couldn't find the way, or will, to begin again. Whatever has caused their dream to derail, they've ultimately written themselves a gigantic permission slip to sit out their own lives.

EVERY SUCCESS STORY
STARTED WITH A

Dream.

That's why I want to share what I've learned with you. I have a mentor's heart, and **I will never buy in to the excuses you may be using for giving up.** I want to help you identify and address whatever is blocking your own success. *Because I know you can ignite your dream and achieve your goals.* Your challenges may be lesser or greater than those I've faced, but one thing is certain: you can learn from everything I have experienced and from everyone who has inspired me.

9

Within these pages are the life-changing lessons and stories of people who have inspired me over the years: friends, mentors, and others I hold in high regard. They've overcome great odds and have become wildly successful.

Why are they in the three percent? Because they followed their dreams and never gave up.

My good friend and client Pavel Datsyuk could have given up after being passed over 657 times in the National Hockey League drafts, but his dream was to be a great hockey player. He worked hard, didn't give up, was finally picked by the Detroit Red Wings and went on to help them win two Stanley Cups. One day he will be inducted into the Hockey Hall of Fame.

Thomas Edison could have given up after 3,000 failed attempts to create the first commercially viable, long-burning incandescent lightbulb, but he kept going, problem solving along the way. Eventually Edison succeeded in creating the first practical lightbulb, cementing his place in history. **These people have inspired me, and I know their stories will inspire you.** During those days or months when you feel your energy and motivation taking a beating, I hope you'll be able to draw strength from their examples and my philosophy of success.

CHOICE
– not circumstance –
determines your success.

Realistically, you can't do everything, but you know that. You cannot be an opera singer if you don't have good pitch, or a famous painter if you have no artistic talent. But most of your dreams—like finding a job you love and making a living doing something that inspires you every day—are realistic goals that everyone can attain. Every morning you have two choices: continue to sleep with your dreams or wake up and chase them. Every day you have to renew your desire to succeed. You can do it, and I want to show you how.

The lessons in this book are the ones I use to persevere, and I use them every day. Like anyone who has achieved substantial success despite being tested by failure and adversity, I've found that

the difference between those who will merely dream of success and those who will successfully reach their dream lies in **attitude** and **action**.

Success must begin in your mind, but you're also charged with taking action because you are the sole architect of your destiny. There's not a lot of hand-holding here; my philosophy runs more along the lines of a swift kick in the pants when you need it.

One of my core principles, of which I often remind people, is

"Success is never owned. It is rented and the rent is due every day!"

Every day I have to prove myself in one way or another, just like everyone should. There is no guarantee of lasting business success. The moment I get it in my head that I'm successful is the day I'm going to hang up my skates and retire. I'm determined not to become complacent, one of those people who has had *former* glory. I want to be useful. That attitude helps ensure that I will never take anything for granted. It also opens the door wide to success.

I believe these lessons can inspire you to relentlessly pursue your dream. If you'll get out of your own way, you can become #1 in whatever defines your passion. So, let's get started. It's time to pay the rent.

section

2

The Rules of Business Success

 Dream it.

 Plan it.

 Do it.

1.

It's not how much you sleep, it's what you do when you're awake.

●

Success means working hard every day and making the necessary sacrifices to accomplish often-challenging goals.

People frequently ask if there is a "secret" to attaining success. The Greek philosopher Socrates had a very simple answer to that question. One day a young man asked him if there was indeed such a secret. Socrates told the man to meet him at a nearby river the following morning. When they met, the philosopher suggested they walk into the water. Socrates surprised his companion by dunking him under and holding him there for several minutes. Finally, he pulled the young man's head out of the water. As he quickly gasped and took a deep breath of air, Socrates asked him, "What did you want the most when you were under water there?" Without hesitating, he replied, "Air." Socrates said, "That is the secret to success. When you want success as badly as you wanted the air, then you will get it. There is no other secret."

The one constant is that every true success story usually begins with a dream, the inspiration to reach seemingly impossible goals. One of my own early dreams of future success

It's essential that you don't let others' definitions of success alter your drive to achieve.

20

occurred as my parents, brother and I stepped off the plane that had taken us from our old home in the Soviet Union to a new one in America. We carried few possessions, and my only money was the 17 cents in my pocket to mail a letter back home to my best friend. My family faced an uncertain future, but I was excited at the potential of our new home and hoped that it would be the first step on my way to achieving the American Dream.

My life has since been made up of many accomplishments—from becoming a top producing salesman to establishing a major residential lending company that has also expanded into publishing, movie production, and a professional celebrity and athlete management group—that many well-meaning people told me were impossible.

It's essential that you don't let others' definitions of success alter your drive to achieve. If the opinion of others is enough to make you quit, then perhaps you're not quite ready for the success about which you dream.

Obviously we learn that achieving success is not an overnight process.

Behind every successful person there are usually several unsuccessful years. You may be one of the lucky ones who enjoys "quick" success, but most people take a steady climb to reach their various goals.

One of the most important lessons I've learned about success from studying great achievers is that **there is no finish line**. If you find you're realizing high aspirations, never be fooled into thinking you have "arrived," as that may lead to arrogance or complacency. How you handle success often determines how long you will hold on to it.

21

Surround yourself with people who dream bigger than you do.

2.

GO BIG OR GO HOME

Whatever you're thinking,

think bigger.

●

You have to **think big** in order to "get ahead."

Soon after arriving in America, I realized that this is a country of big thinkers with supersized visions. I adjusted my own ways of viewing things and tried to adopt some of the best practices of successful people, such as Henry Ford, Ray Kroc, and Bill Gates. Among other things, their common characteristics include supreme confidence, a thorough knowledge of their industry's potential challenges and solutions, and "the glass is three-quarters full" philosophy. These and many other accomplished entrepreneurs always stretch themselves and take bold actions.

When I consider big thinkers, I always recall the story of San Francisco businessman Amadeo Giannini, who lived during the early part of the twentieth century. He opened his San Francisco Bay business in an old saloon and catered to the hardworking immigrants that others would not serve at the time.

But shortly after Giannini set up shop, the Great Earthquake of 1906 struck. Homes were reduced to rubble. Rather than leave the area as many did, he decided that he would help members of the community by lending them money, proclaiming that San Francisco would be the first area to rise from the ashes. Since most of the banks in the area had been destroyed and were unable to lend money, Giannini set up a plank across two barrels at the corner of an intersection. There he collected deposits and made rebuilding loans to businesses based on a handshake. He got the economy moving again. Little did anyone know at the time that these loans and deposits would form the basis of the portfolio that would later become Bank of America, one of the largest financial institutions in the world.

Giannini didn't invent commercial lending. But what he did do was think about the enormous opportunity before him and spring into action as soon as he could get that plank across those barrels. He accomplished what those who were giving up thought impossible, by thinking—and acting quickly—on a

26

grand scale. He wasn't concerned about how he was going to replace the windows in his saloon. He was concerned about how to salvage the city's economy—and in turn laid the foundation of a banking empire. He accomplished what others thought was impossible by not being afraid to think on a grand scale.

I must admit that some of my own early career moves might have been a little grandiose, but the overall approach has generally worked to my advantage.

Businesspeople often say it's wise to include a "big idea" in a plan or proposal—something that is exceptionally distinctive. But from my perspective, the entire plan or goal should be based on an ambitious vision. You won't be able to develop aggressive goals and achieve huge results by thinking small.

You should have goals so big that you are uncomfortable telling your friends about them.

Mark Zuckerberg had a big goal. In 2004, the 19-year-old Harvard sophomore partnered with his college roommates and a fellow Harvard student to found Facebook. Today, Mark Zuckerberg's net worth is $51.5 billion, Dustin Moskovitz—$9.8 billion, Eduardo Saverin—$7.2 billion, Chris Hughes—$450 million, and Andrew McCollum—$18 million. They didn't let their youth or inexperience stop them. Nor should you. Never be afraid to try something new. Remember, amateurs built the ark; professionals built the Titanic.

When I started in the lending business I strived to be the best, determined to become the top loan officer in the country. That was a big goal, which I only shared with a few people because I knew they would think it was out of reach.

I encourage our managers and other employees to think of their most innovative ideas. There are no limitations. Obviously some of the "over the top" concepts may not be feasible to actually implement, but along the way this approach leads to some dramatic results. An interesting phenomenon occurs: thinking beyond and around limitations becomes a habit. Apply this same concept to your own daily behavior, and I guarantee you'll eventually become a big league thinker. You have to remind yourself:

"Today I will **do** what others won't do so tomorrow I can do **what others can't.**"

It's not about being the best.

It's about being

better than you were yesterday.

3.

Focus on your future, live in the present, and learn from your past.

•

You'll have a much greater chance for long-term success by constantly focusing directly on what you want in life.

Lack of clarity is one of the major stumbling blocks to success. Too often people rush into something without being fully prepared. They start with an exciting idea, but haven't thought it all the way through. As a result, they may be unsure of their purpose or direction.

Without a clear direction, you can quickly wander off course, which leads to delays reaching your destination, whether it's an immediate or long-term project. I always like to remind people that "A man without a vision for his future always returns to his past."

In the early phase of my career, I took a few missteps. I definitely had the desire, but wasn't quite sure how to get there. I was impatient and overlooked some of the fundamentals necessary to be successful. I also had to redefine my purpose—for example, was I seeking a long-term career, or to become financially secure at a

The harder you work, ◄ ◄ ◄

► ► ► the luckier you get.

young age, or some combination? Once I was absolutely clear of what I wanted and how to get there, I was on a fast track and never looked back.

Many people start out with a clearly defined purpose, but then their focus becomes blurred. Well-known former Dallas Cowboys football coach Jimmy Johnson had an opportunity to share an important pregame lesson with his players. "I told them that if I laid a two-by-four plank across the room, everybody there would walk across it and not fall, because our focus would be that we were going to walk that two-by-four," Johnson said of this motivational talk. "But if I put that same two-by-four plank 10 stories high between two buildings only a few would make it, because the focus would be on failing. Focus is everything. The team that is more focused today is the team that will win this game."

Johnson told his team not to be distracted by the crowds, the media, or the possibility of losing, but to focus on each play of the game itself just as if it were a good practice session. The Cowboys obviously listened carefully to their coach's talk. They had a decisive win that day. This kind of coaching helped Johnson and the Dallas Cowboys win two Super Bowls.

Some people find it easier to develop "clarity of purpose" than others. They are able to articulate their goal and pathway from the very beginning and can then focus on their objective with laser-like concentration. However, others have a more difficult time with what seems to be a simple process.

36

> Whenever I talk to **new** employees worldwide, or our celebrity and sports agency clients, I ask them what their **short- and long-term goals** are.

I encourage them to write this in a statement of a few sentences, and then reread it a few days later. They frequently see that their initial Purpose Statement isn't as clear as they intended, which then gives them an opportunity to rethink and revise it. It is a powerful exercise that you can adapt to your own business and personal lives.

Not everyone will see your purpose and goals the way you do. Sometimes the people around you won't understand your journey. They don't need to—it's not for them.

Time is money.

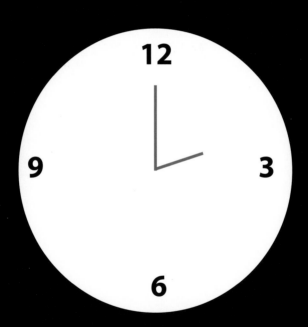

4.

Lack of time is actually lack of priorities.

•

You must know what your **priorities** are.

Priorities are more than a daily or weekly "to do" list; rather, they refer to those things that are most important to us professionally and personally. They guide us as we establish a set of goals and develop a framework with which to accomplish them. And as we remain focused on our priorities, they also help us continue to make necessary adjustments in order to reach our goals.

Being at the "top of their game" is a major priority for many people, as it has been for me since the day I entered the workforce at age 16. As I tell most people, **my number one rule is "Don't be #2."** However, part of that is developing patience, and improving incrementally until you've reached the highest possible mark. Early on I realized that "it's not always about being the best, it's about being better than you were yesterday." One of my other early priorities was to not be the smartest person in the room. I always wanted to be open-minded, willing to learn whatever I could from mentors and fellow employees.

Early on I realized that "it's not always about being the best, it's about being better than you were yesterday."

Brain surgeon Ben Carson's mother made her son's education a priority. Sonya Carson was an illiterate woman with only a third grade education who married at age 13. She later found herself a single mother raising her son in poverty. Wanting more for Ben, she insisted he read two books per week. Her priorities became his, and he went on to earn a medical degree, publish several books, and even make a bid for the presidency of the United States. Sonya Carson used a library card to raise a brain surgeon. Never underestimate the power of the human mind.

Abraham Lincoln's determination and perseverance is another excellent example of focused priorities. In addition to ending the Civil War, Lincoln's number one priority was ending slavery. As the war continued, his obsession with ending slavery

DREAMS DON'T WORK
UNLESS YOU DO.

included 1863's Emancipation Proclamation, using the U.S. Army to protect escaped slaves, encouraging border states to outlaw slavery, and prompting Congress to enact the Thirteenth Amendment to the Constitution of the United States. He fought critics in both parties who either didn't support his mission or were skeptical that he could accomplish it. Lincoln remained true to his priorities.

Our priorities certainly evolve. As a newly arrived immigrant to America, my main priority was fitting in with my high school classmates. Later it was graduating from college and finding business success, then establishing my own firm and ensuring that it would thrive, rather than simply survive, during difficult times.

We often hear people say "get your priorities straight," meaning that they may question someone else's values. But I believe that should only apply to unprofessional or otherwise poor behavior. I'm usually most inspired by those who have developed a set of ethical principles and don't let others dictate what their priorities should be. As I often tell people, **"Don't worry about what I'm doing. Just worry about what you're not doing**, and remember that the difference between excellence and mediocrity is commitment."

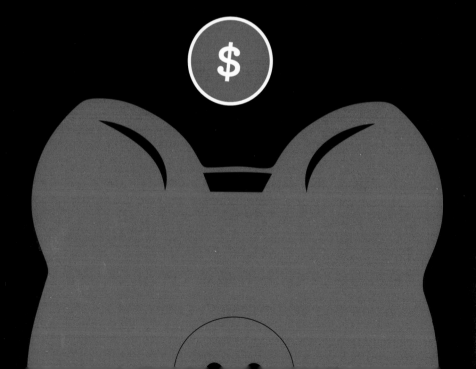

TWO THIRDS

of the world's billionaires **made their** fortunes **from** scratch.

5.

Eighty-six percent of millionaires are self-made.

•

The only way we will reach our full potential—in our work and personal lives—is by raising the performance bar.

We won't get there by maintaining the status quo or lowering the bar when we have an especially difficult month or year. You have to shoot for the moon, because even if you miss, you'll land among the stars. You'll still achieve greater overall results than if you hadn't pushed yourself, and along the way you'll have made the necessary adjustments for future growth.

People say, "The sky is the limit," when talking about someone's potential accomplishments. However, I believe you can amend that to, "The sky isn't the limit, but rather your mind is." Because of a lack of self-confidence, someone else's perception of our abilities, or another reason, there is a tendency for people to limit themselves by applying self-imposed restrictions.

When Morris Markin arrived at Ellis Island from Russia in the early 1900s, he spoke no English and was unable to pay the bond required to enter the United States. A janitor there loaned him the $25 required for the bond. Even then Markin was clearly ambitious, learning how to set high expectations in his new home country. From New York he traveled to Chicago to live with his uncle. He later held several jobs as an errand boy, including work for a tailor who taught him the trade. Markin worked hard and was able to save enough money to bring his seven brothers and two sisters to America. He and one of his brothers subsequently opened a factory that made pants under government contracts during World War I, and their company was quite successful. In 1921, Markin entered the automobile business when he acquired an auto body manufacturing company, and later a failed automobile manufacturer, a defunct chassis plant, and a body plant in Kalamazoo, Michigan. Markin relocated the entire operation to Kalamazoo and in 1922 formed the Checker Cab Manufacturing Company. By refusing to set limits, Markin was able to achieve the remarkable success about which many others only dream.

Today I will do what others won't so tomorrow I can do what others can't.

Many professions force their members to regularly surpass their previous performance levels. Salespeople must continue to increase their annual volume. However, the most successful people have learned to raise the bar on their own. They are always looking for ways to exceed last year's performance. When I was first striving to be one of my industry's top loan officers, it was apparent that I'd have to push myself beyond what my sales manager expected. Even when I formed my own company, I often set overly ambitious targets, but that enabled me to continue reaching higher.

It can be a little difficult to know just how far to raise the bar, but if you're in doubt, make smaller increases until you reach a reasonable level. But don't ever "settle" for less than you're capable of doing.

If you're not achieving what you want, don't lower your expectations. Instead, you need to raise your standards.

Surpassing your limits can also be applied to your personal life. You just have to determine what you want to accomplish—and then raise your own bar and leap over it. Remember that reaching higher to achieve success is supposed to be hard. If it was easy, everybody would be doing it.

Do something today that your future self will thank you for.

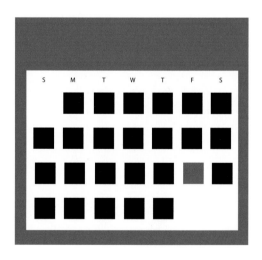

6.

DO IT NOW

One year from now, you'll wish you had started today.

●

There is no room for procrastinators in a fast paced, results-oriented organization.

"Get this done" and "we need it yesterday" are frequently heard directives in most companies.

I have been fortunate to learn from a number of successful, forward-thinking professors, entrepreneurs, and other professionals. One of the early lessons that helped me to become a top producing salesman was a slight variation on a well-known quote:

"Don't put off until tomorrow what you can do right now."

Decisiveness and immediacy enable us to get more accomplished—faster. Remember, the difference between could and did is action. There are plenty of people who say, "I could do that," but few who are able to say "I did it," before moving on to their next task.

MY BIGGEST REGRETS ARE

THE OPPORTUNITIES I DIDN'T TAKE.

Many people complain they don't have enough time to finish a specific job. However, a lack of time is actually a lack of prioritization. **If you have established priorities, you will make the time to get things done.** I have a longstanding practice of not stopping work until I have finished my "To Do" list. That may even mean when we're "off the clock" and in a social setting.

One late night I was relaxing at a bar with some coworkers. As we told stories and planned for the next day, my phone rang; it was a transfer from the office sales line. A couple of my colleagues shook their heads, encouraging me to ignore the call. However,

I never stop looking for opportunities,

so there was no way I'd let it go to voicemail. I introduced myself, and asked the caller how I could help. He was an airline pilot who had just landed after a long international flight. The pilot explained that he had been thinking about a potential home purchase, and was anxious to talk about his desired home

59

loan. Of course, I hadn't expected a sales call at 2:15 a.m. But, rather than delay the discussion until the following day, I quickly took his application on what was available—a cocktail napkin.

I had his loan in process the following morning and it closed in record time. The pilot subsequently remarked how impressed he was that I had made myself available to take his loan application when it was convenient for *him*. He soon began referring customers to me. It was another reminder that **there is always time to start or finish a job.**

Some people prefer the common strategy of starting their day by working on a few easy things, enabling them to ease into the daily schedule. I disagree with this approach. I believe that you can motivate yourself and get the day off to a great start by tackling a few of the difficult tasks first. Once you've done that, it feels like you can handle anything.

I still have that framed, beer-stained napkin in my office, reminding me that opportunities arrive 24/7 and you always have to be ready for them.

Having a sense of urgency is what will separate you from 90 percent of the people who read books and attend seminars but never see significant results. A sense of urgency generates action. So, do it now.

Everything
you need
to become #1
lies within you.

Your Signature

7.

Work so hard that one day your signature will be called an autograph.

●

A quitter **never wins** and a winner **never quits.**

I've seen winners in sports, business, academics, and other areas. I've watched many of our athlete clients, observed Olympic athletes challenge one another, and been impressed to see determined businesspeople succeed in the face of what seem to be impossible odds. One quality they all share is simply never giving up. They may not succeed at everything, but they do not quit. If they stumble, they rise and keep competing. They rarely make excuses and do everything possible to avoid stopping short of the finish line.

At the 2014 Winter Olympics in Sochi, I was privileged to see numerous examples of the winning spirit. One of the most inspiring stories was actually about someone who lost. During the finals of the men's cross-country skiing sprint, Russian skier Anton Gafarov crashed hard. As he got up, Gafarov and everyone nearby could see he had a broken ski. He was devastated to get to this point and not be able to continue the race, but he struggled to push on, obviously far behind his competitors. Spectators and television viewers could see the determination and frustration on his face. Then seemingly out of nowhere, the coach of the Canadian team approached—with a new ski. He helped Gafarov replace the ski and then quickly returned to his own place on the sidelines. While he obviously didn't win, Gafarov also didn't have to be viewed as a quitter. "I wanted him to have dignity as he crossed the finish line," said Justin Wadsworth, the Canadian coach.

I've also seen many people who could be considered quitters, because they gave up during difficult situations. They may have been as smart as the winners, but they didn't have the drive to follow through. They didn't realize that pain is temporary, but quitting lasts forever.

I've often thought that 97 percent of the people who quit too soon are employed by the three percent who never gave up.

Part of being a winner is being able to deal with less-than-positive results. I remind myself that in every challenging situation, I either win—or I learn from the unsuccessful outcome. But I am still committed to the win. **I'm never satisfied unless I've competed as hard as I can.**

Winners also know the importance of the preparation involved for an athletic event or business deal. It's often not just the will to win, but the will to prepare to win that can make the difference. Amateurs practice until they get it "right." Professionals practice until they can't get it "wrong."

The key is to give everything you have every time.

Professional and amateur athletes alike insist that they "left it all on the field." They did everything possible to win the game and wouldn't have done anything differently. We should all strive to have a competitor's attitude and determination as we pursue every one of our daily goals.

PRODUCTIVITY

is never an accident.

It is the result of

a plan in action.

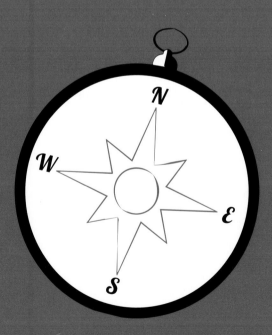

8.

CHART YOUR COURSE

A goal without a plan is just a wish.

●

Benjamin Franklin was obviously right when he said, "If you fail to plan, you are planning to fail."

Most people wouldn't leave on a major trip without a map or directions. Why, then, do some think they can achieve an ambitious goal or other undertaking without a plan? Without a plan you'll most likely wander off course.

One of my favorite quotes is, "Excuses will always be there, but opportunities won't, and you won't get many choice opportunities without a plan."

The first step is to have a set of goals—for a career, family life, personal interests, and other areas. If you're looking for some fresh ideas, make a list of the people you admire and what makes them amazing. Then go out and become those things yourself.

Stay true to your goals.
If the plan doesn't work, change
the plan—not the goal.

Goals and plans often seem unattainable, unless you're especially motivated. In 1976, Arnold Schwarzenegger was a successful bodybuilder, but definitely not a well-known celebrity. One day he was talking with a newspaper reporter who asked, "Now that you've retired from bodybuilding, what do you plan to do next?"

In his distinctive Austrian accent, Schwarzenegger shared his plan in a confident, matter-of-fact way: "I'm going to be the #1 movie star in Hollywood."

The reporter was most likely shocked at Schwarzenegger's plan. After all, how could this over-confident body builder who spoke poor English think that he could be a successful actor, let alone a box office draw?

The reporter was curious about how Schwarzenegger aimed to make his dream come true. What kind of plan would help him

Shoot for the **MOON.**

Even if you miss,

you'll land among

THE STARS.

achieve that seemingly elusive goal? Schwarzenegger replied, "I'll do it the same way I became the #1 body builder in the world. **What I do is to create a vision of who I want to be**, then I start living like that person in my mind as if it were already true."

That type of plan doesn't necessarily work for everybody, but it made sense to Schwarzenegger. He eventually did act in American movies and for a time was the highest paid movie star in Hollywood. Of course, he also became the Governor of California. **Goals only become permanent when they're formal;** otherwise they are often vague generalizations. Write them down.

Seeing goals in your own handwriting has a powerful effect.

You don't need a PowerPoint presentation or a fancy binder. You can simply have visual reminders of your plan on a computer screensaver or desk sign.

Part of the reason my early business career stalled was because I didn't have a written plan. After a great deal of soul searching, I realized, among other things, the need to be better prepared and that a simple "To Do" list was no longer sufficient. Organizing my goals into a written plan made a substantial difference. There's absolutely no way I could have become a successful salesman and then establish a major corporation without quarterly, annual, three, five and ten-year plans. I now use my smart phone and a notepad to make daily adjustments and I don't go to bed until I have a written plan of action for the next day.

The future belongs to those who prepare for it today.

While you debated
whether the glass
is empty or full,
I sold it.

9

Since most people operate inside the box, the competition outside the box is very low.

●

Good luck is what happens when preparation meets opportunity. **Bad luck** is what happens when lack of preparation meets a challenge.

It's easy and less risky to react rather than act, to passively wait for things to happen instead of making them happen yourself. That's why it's important to be proactive. Being proactive means that you are willing and committed to get out in front, and take the necessary steps to achieve short- and long-term goals.

Opportunities often pass us by because we aren't willing to be the first ones to move.

The problem is that **you lose so many chances by waiting for the "right time."** My own biggest regrets are the opportunities I didn't take. Motivational speaker and consultant Denis Waitley said, "Losers let it happen; winners make it happen."

Richard Branson is definitely one of those who makes it "happen." Branson has dyslexia and had a poor academic record as a student. On his last day at school, his headmaster told him he would either end up in prison or become a millionaire. Branson actually became a billionaire, in large part because he has been one of the world's most proactive entrepreneurs.

Branson was only 16 when he launched his first business enterprise—a magazine called *Student*. He continued making bold moves from that point on, looking for opportunities that others didn't see or were too timid to develop. They have included Virgin Records, Virgin Atlantic, Virgin Mobile, Virgin Fuels, and Virgin Galactic, a space tourism company. He hasn't stopped yet.

Andrew Ference used this technique to get into the National Hockey League. The 18-year-old Ference loved to play hockey, but scouts weren't impressed with the young defenseman. He wasn't invited for testing to qualify for the 1997 NHL draft. Ference refused to accept that he wouldn't be able to play for the league—his dream—so on his own he contacted the same organization that the NHL's Central Scouting Bureau invited other prospects to go through, and underwent the physical testing to prove the scouts wrong. He then faxed his test results to every team's general manager with a letter stating, "I am looking forward to proving myself this fall at my first NHL training camp, for whatever team is prepared to give me that opportunity. I guarantee that the team that has the confidence to draft me will not regret their decision."

The Pittsburgh Penguins took a chance and drafted him in the 1997 NHL draft. For nearly two decades, Ference had a stellar NHL hockey career with several teams, and was also chosen as a team captain. Because he was proactive and *didn't give up*, Ference has been able to live out his dream. In fact, he has his name engraved on the Stanley Cup. What if he had listened to critics and never pursued his goals?

There are numerous instances where otherwise astute business leaders, athletes or others missed a significant opportunity to make a bold and profitable move. Atari founder Nolan Bushnell was one of Steve Jobs' first bosses and could have invested $50,000 in seed money in Apple, but decided against it. Had he done so, Bushnell would have owned a sizeable portion of Apple. During his spare time while working at Hewlett Packard in the 1970s, Steve Wozniak created a PC. Several times he asked HP executives to manufacture his computer, but it seems they weren't interested. So Wozniak joined his friend Steve Jobs to start Apple.

Gold Star's own success has been largely based on having a great team of people and making bold moves. Whether it has been by expanding rather than cutting back during difficult times, by developing subsidiary companies such as publishing and movie production, or by creating a unique working environment for employees, we've strived to stay ahead of others. We generally avoid the "wait and see" approach before taking action.

You can sometimes get bogged down with the details of reviewing and fine-tuning plans before acting, but if you keep counting the steps you'll never get anywhere. When meeting with new employees, I emphasize the importance of being proactive. I'll say "While you debated whether the glass is half empty or full, I sold it."

Being **proactive** often means you have to **jump** into unfamiliar territory.

Standing on the edge is not as safe, but trust me, the view is much better. Be bold, take a risk, and act first.

Don't aspire to be the best
ON THE TEAM.
Aspire to be the best
FOR THE TEAM.

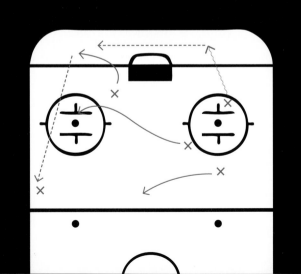

10.

IT'S A TEAM SPORT

Teamwork divides the task and multiplies the success.

●

Talent might win you the game, but it takes teamwork to win the championship.

Part of your success can be attributed to collaboration with others. There is generally no such thing as a "lone wolf." You must depend on the cooperation of co-workers, business colleagues, family members and friends.

Nearly everything I have accomplished so far has been the result of a group effort. Before starting Gold Star I worked for three major banks. If they expected me to close a certain number of transactions, my goal was to double it, and to make that organization better in the process. I was always aware that wouldn't have been possible without the other team members' support.

The late Steve Jobs' innovations and other noteworthy achievements included his concept of teamwork, which he thought highly of and explained with this analogy: "We had a lot of great ideas when we started," Jobs said. "But what I've always felt that a team of people doing something they really believe in is like ... when I was a young kid there was a widowed man that lived up the street. He was in his eighties ... And I got to know him a little bit."

Jobs told the story of visiting the old man who had used a rock tumbler to polish stones. He considered that an ideal metaphor for a team working on a project. "It's that through the team, through that group of incredibly talented people bumping up against each other, having arguments, having fights sometimes, making some noise, and working together, they polish each other and they polish the ideas, and what comes out are these really beautiful stones," said Jobs.

You may not have a formal team to support you. However, you still have a group of people with whom you work—even though you may all have equal standing. Consider colleagues and associates as team members who can help you reach your job-related goals. Include them in your planning process when appropriate, and listen to their suggestions. You can also help them reach their goals.

From my early days at McDonald's, to the corporate boardroom, I've looked for ways to build and nurture teams.

I've learned that you shouldn't aspire to be the best on the team. You must aspire to be the best for the team.

89

If you're simply trying to be the best on the team, you don't leave much room for other people to grow and to lead. You'll find that spotlight-stealers and credit-takers don't typically rise up the leadership ladder. They are more interested in their own agenda than in the team's potential, and it shows. It's often said that if service is beneath you, leadership is beyond you.

True leaders don't create followers; they create more leaders. That's why we look for new employees who have the potential to become leaders; they can continue helping us grow while they develop their careers. The great ones want to be coaches and get better every day.

Our wonderful country, fueled by capitalism, is the epitome

ENTREPRENEURSHIP

is living a few years of your life

LIKE MOST PEOPLE WON'T

so you can live the rest of your life

LIKE MOST PEOPLE CAN'T.

of teamwork, a topic that came up in an interesting conversation I had. A man I was with looked at a Cadillac Escalade and said, "I wonder how many people could have been fed for the cost of that car." I replied, "I am not sure. It fed a lot of families of the people in Michigan and Texas who built it; it fed the people who made the tires; it fed the people who made the components; it fed the people in the copper mine who mined the copper for the wires; and it fed the people who made the trucks that haul the copper ore. That's the difference between capitalism and welfare mentality. When you buy something, you put money in people's pockets and give them dignity for their skills."

You also **create teamwork**, and out of that can come amazing things.

Someone is sitting in the shade today because someone planted a tree a long time ago.

Keep self-talk positive.

11.

DREAMS DON'T WORK
UNLESS YOU DO

Don't tell people your dreams; show them.

•

Dreams have inspired incredible inventions and led to highly successful careers.

One of my early dreams after arriving in America was to be a bagger at a local grocery store so I could earn enough to buy the red Pontiac Fiero I saw in a newspaper ad. I later dreamed of becoming a manager at McDonald's, getting a white-collar job, then becoming a bank vice president before turning 40, starting my own company, and eventually writing a book. In some ways, I consider myself to be just a dreamer who never stopped believing that one day his dreams would become reality.

But dreams don't work unless you do. When you dream of something special—becoming a pro athlete, doctor or business owner—you have to take action or otherwise it's just an unfulfilled wish. Some people dream of success, while others wake up and work hard for it. I've learned from Walt Disney who once said, "All our dreams can come true, if we have the courage to pursue them." It's easy to dream about something in the future; the key is to develop a plan and follow it, just as he did with the creation of Disneyland.

Some people dream of success, while others wake up and work hard for it.

Colin Powell, one of the people I most admire, wanted to soar beyond his humble upbringing, and he became an Army General and U.S. Secretary of State. He also knew the work involved in realizing your dreams: **"A dream doesn't become reality through magic; it takes sweat, determination, and hard work."**

I have become much more aggressive about chasing my dreams, rather than merely following them. This has required a significant sacrifice of long hours and overcoming many obstacles, but has certainly been worth it.

One of the biggest obstacles to realizing our dreams is listening too closely when other people tell us we're being

SELF-MOTIVATION
AND HARD WORK

DRIVE YOUR SUCCESS

unrealistic, that it will take too much to achieve them, and that we should lower our expectations. The risk in listening to naysayers is that your own thoughts may begin to echo what they're saying. Be careful about what you tell yourself, as the person in charge of your destiny is listening. I am always striving to **keep "self-talk" positive**.

Howard Schultz's dream was to have a nationwide chain of upscale coffee shops, but he was told repeatedly this was an unrealistic concept. More than 240 banks turned down his request for financing. If Schultz had listened to and believed the critics, we wouldn't have Starbucks on nearly every corner. Don't let small minds tell you that your dreams are too big. Only you know how important the dream is and how determined you are to achieve it.

Joshua Riehl dreamed of making a movie about the Russian Five, the legendary ice hockey pros who played for the Detroit Red Wings in the 1990s. He spent seven years trying to obtain the financing to produce the film, but was unable to secure backers who were willing to take a chance on an inexperienced director. Riehl refused to give up and even relocated to Detroit to be closer to the Red Wings archives, which would help him complete the research for the movie. We were later introduced and I was incredibly impressed with his enthusiasm and unwavering belief in the dream to make this movie. Gold Star Films made the excellent decision to produce *The Russian Five*.

Some people **want** their dreams to happen, some **wish** they would happen, and **others make** them happen.

The difference between 'could' and 'did' is action.

12.

Some dream about it.

I work for it.

●

The American Dream of getting an education, finding a good job, and enjoying prosperity is achievable; but only if you work hard for it. I know from experience that the dream exists.

When I got my first real American job at a local McDonald's restaurant, it was a lifeline for me—an immigrant who couldn't speak English who desperately wanted hope for the future. I knew that "flipping burgers" was not beneath my dignity. I had a different word for it. I called it an "opportunity." Since I was 16 and in high school, I had to split my shift in half. I would start work at 5:00 a.m. each day, then rush to school, and finally return to work to finish the last five hours of my eight-hour shift. I was up every day at 4:00 a.m. so I could get to McDonald's on time, and often not return home until

I don't stop when I am tired,

I STOP WHEN I AM DONE

after 9:00 p.m. Adding this schedule to my homework made for an extremely long day, but I was determined to make it work.

I was so appreciative of my McDonald's job that I actually painted the Golden Arches on my bedroom wall. It was an impulsive move, but my parents didn't mind. It was a sign of the pride I felt for the company that had allowed me to work there.

I discovered the necessity of hard work—landscaping, at a tire store, selling door-to-door, and McDonald's. I had no option but to create **a solid work ethic**, and it has served me well.

I knew that there were other people who could replace me. "Work like there is someone working 24 hours a day to take it all away from you," said Mark Cuban. I didn't consider the work drudgery, although it wasn't especially exciting or rewarding. I believed that by working hard I would eventually achieve my dream of a successful career that would inspire and reward me.

People often talk about having luck as a key part of success. But good fortune is only possible if you first make the effort.

Hard work puts you in a place where good luck can find you.

Haben Girma learned early in life about working hard. Born both deaf and blind to a refugee mother who escaped from Eritrea to the U.S., Girma had to learn early in life to overcome boundaries. After graduating magna cum laude from Lewis and Clark College in 2010, she realized she would need a higher education to get anywhere in the work world, so she decided to go to law school and became the first deaf-blind person to graduate from Harvard. She has earned recognition as the White House "Champion of Change," is a *Forbes* 30 Under 30 leader, and is an internationally acclaimed accessibility leader and disability rights advocate. She works as a civil rights attorney. Haben definitely had some challenges to overcome. But, instead of looking at herself as a victim, she found ways to overcome her disabilities, and through hard work and tenacity she cleared the path for others to follow.

106

After a series of obstacles, including being rejected for an engineering job at Toyota Motor Corporation, Soichiro Honda began making his own scooters at home. Encouraged by his neighbors, he eventually started his own business. He is the holder of 100 patents and founder of the Honda Motor Corporation.

To achieve goals, you must **work hard**, be determined, **juggle more** than you can handle, and **work when others sleep**. I've learned to accept that I'm only as good as my next client and my next deal.

No matter how you feel—**get up, dress up, show up, and never give up.** Most people are not willing to work hard enough to achieve all of their goals. Don't be like most people.

There are no
DISCOUNTS
on the price of
SUCCESS

13.

Hard work puts you in a place where good luck can find you.

Excuses will always be there for you.
Opportunity won't.

You will hear people say, "I don't have enough support to finish the project" . . . "I need more time" . . . "I can't work without special resources."

Every excuse is a personal debt; eventually they will foreclose on your dreams.

While you're waiting for the ideal work environment, your competitors are passing you by. They have figured out how to get the job done with what they have. **The key is to make the absolute best of the current situation**, be successful at every level, and meanwhile try to acquire the extra resources.

After working at several jobs during and after high school, my goal was to have a white-collar job. One day while still in college, I was waiting for a bus and noticed several well-dressed men and women entering a major bank's corporate office in Ann Arbor, Michigan. I thought **this would be a great way to kick-start my entry into the business world**, but knew I'd need a suit to interview for an entry-level position there. Not having appropriate attire, my options were to wait until I could afford to purchase a new suit, such as those worn by the men entering the bank, or find a used one.

Unwilling to wait, the next day I went to the nearby Salvation Army store and purchased what seemed to be a decent suit and tie for two dollars. I arranged an interview with the bank and wore my "new" clothes that day.

I may not have overwhelmed them with my fashion sense, but I did get my first job in the financial services profession. I faked it so I could get a jumpstart on my career and to this day am amazed and appreciative that I got such an opportunity.

I realized life isn't always about finding yourself, but rather about creating yourself.

When I started Gold Star Mortgage Financial Group with my

life savings of $3,500, I was faced with many challenges. We were up against much larger, well-established businesses and in the midst of a sluggish economy. My first office was a small room that had been used as a storage closet by the previous tenant. Instead of focusing on ways we didn't measure up to our glossy competition, we developed our niche based on what they weren't doing well, and focused on high volume at discount prices. We also began catering to the immigrant communities that felt they'd been underserved by area banks.

I realized life isn't always about finding yourself, but rather about creating yourself.

Rather than spend money on larger office space, I spent my energy and resources on locating like-minded, multilingual loan officers who would share my servant-lender vision, and soon there were four of us packed into that tiny office. Fluent in eight languages between us, our conversations sounded very much like the United Nations on a busy Friday afternoon. I learned early on that it's always more important to invest in people than real estate, and like Amadeo Giannini, who collected deposits for his "bank" from a wooden plank across two barrels, we didn't wait for lavish accommodations and perfect conditions.

You might think our early customers would be concerned that Gold Star was a brand new company with a 24-year-old president. Or that they would turn up their nose at our tiny office. That was not the case, as we gave them something far more important than a spectacular view from the tenth floor. **We gave them our respect.** We gave them highly personalized, beyond-the-call service, exceptional pricing, and the knowledge that we were looking out for their best interests. We fought like tigers on their behalf. Not one of them would remember the weak coffee we served in Styrofoam cups. But all of them remember the feeling of being respected. I'm proud to say that the service level and the sincere respect we afford each and every customer became our most important core value, and that value is the rock-solid platform of all of the Gold Star companies.

You too will reach your destinations faster if you don't wait until conditions are perfect. **When a window of opportunity opens, don't pull down the shade.**

No one is born successful.
Success or failure
is only determined by
where you stop.

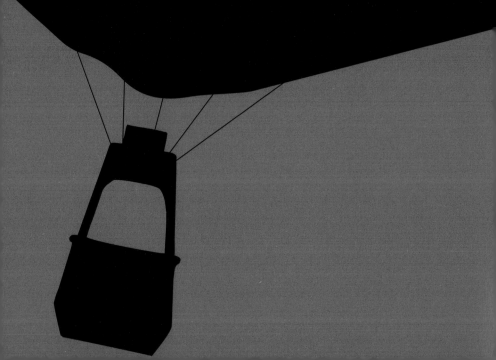

14.

The distance between dreams and reality is called action.

●

Plan your work, then work your plan.

For some it's a reality check—that point when we have to stop what we're doing and determine if we are headed in the wrong direction.

You won't achieve ultimate success if you're treading water . . . unsure if your goals are realistic . . . wondering why you missed a recent promotion . . . feeling overwhelmed with your current responsibilities . . . or are worrying that your supervisor is looking over your shoulder, waiting for your performance to improve.

Some big mistakes have occurred by people wavering on decisions; sometimes you need to take chances. In 1998, Yahoo had the opportunity to acquire Google for $1 million, but didn't make the buy. In 2002 Yahoo realized its mistake and offered Google $3 billion, but now Google wanted $5 billion, which Yahoo refused to pay. In 2008, Microsoft offered $50 billion to acquire Yahoo. Yahoo rejected the offer. In 2016, Yahoo was sold for $5 billion, and the current value of Google is around $545 billion.

You may not like the situation but you need to find a remedy. It's your responsibility to figure out the cure. Rather than waiting for someone to give you the solution, figure out what has to be done now, not in a week or two. The next step you take can have a major impact on your short- and long-term success. You'll either continue in the fog—frustrated at your situation but feeling powerless to solve it— or force yourself to face the difficulty and move on.

You can't always change the people or circumstances in your life, but you can always change your response.

A reality check often means making some hard choices. Obviously you have to objectively analyze what's really causing you to be so stressed or otherwise unable to succeed, and actually do something about it. You may have to clear the air with your supervisor, make a job change, or address personal issues that are blocking your progress. Life begins at the end of your comfort zone.

Some people are extremely successful, or on the way to achieving their most important goals. However, most aren't, because they're stalled and unable to make a move that will get them closer to even modest contentment. Such was the case with a woman who called me soon after I had been interviewed on a TV program.

I could sense both frustration and relief in her voice. She was discouraged at her past, but apparently more positive about the future, because she had her own reality check that led her to make a major decision. She had six children, was on welfare for several years, and hadn't been able to see past the bleakness of her family's condition. "For a long time, it seemed hopeless," she told me. "But then I began considering the options. The real decision came after I heard you speak." She said that listening to me talk about working hard to **realize goals** and **chasing our dreams** motivated her to act. She was

Some days I'm humble,
some days I struggle,
but every day I hustle.

inspired to make a change, and started by returning to college to get her degree.

I won't take the credit for the change this woman made; I merely provided her the "kick start" to move forward. The reality check confirmed that she would go in a different direction in order to leave the uncomfortable place she and her children were in. **She learned that choice, not circumstance, determines success.**

A reality check is often the push that will get you back on track to the next level of success. But you have to be ready and willing to act. Are you?

Stop chasing the money.

START CHASING BEING THE BEST.

15.

Don't pick a job with great vacation time. Pick one that doesn't need escaping from.

If you love what you do, you'll never work a day in your life.

Unfortunately, from my experience, very few people follow this advice. They work at mind-numbing jobs in which they have no interest and remain unable to take control of their own happiness and fulfillment.

I am absolutely passionate about my work. I love helping people, selling ideas, assisting employees, and facing new challenges. I haven't taken a "sick day" since 1998 because I love my job. I'm as enthusiastic as the day I started.

You have a great opportunity to be someone who loves what you do. **Imagine waking up every day, excited to go to work.** If you don't feel that way now, you need to do something about it.

Some people are fortunate enough to find their passion at an early age. Bill Gates wrote his first computer software at the age of 13. Later he founded Microsoft and changed the world by putting his software program on almost every computer out there. Gates has been passionate about his work from the beginning.

Not everyone feels such passion early in life. Like many others, it took me a while to find something about which I could be passionate. My mother wanted me to be a doctor, but I knew that wasn't the right profession for me. I thought that my McDonald's management experience might lead to running my own restaurant. I eventually found my way to the financial services field, and celebrity and athlete representation, and discovered my passion: selling.

If you aren't content at what you are currently doing, then you need to ask yourself what will make you happy. You may need to find a different career, because ultimately **it's your responsibility to find the passion in your work**. Money shouldn't be your prime motivator. Chris Gardner, the former homeless man who became an entrepreneur, corporate CEO, and author of the *Pursuit of Happyness*, said, "Find something you love. Something that gets

BEING ON THE EDGE IS NOT AS SAFE

but the view is better

you so excited you can't wait to get out of bed in the morning. Forget about money. Be happy." You won't truly be rich until you have something money can't buy. You also shouldn't be overly concerned about vacation time.

If your job is simply something you tolerate between vacations, you're in the wrong job.

Meanwhile, until you find the ideal place, give 110 percent to every job you have. Always do your best. No matter what job you have in life, your success will be determined 5% by your academic credentials, 15% by your professional experience, and 80% by your communication skills.

Steve Jobs once said, "The only way to do great work is to love what you do. If you haven't found it yet, keep looking. Don't settle . . . Have the courage to follow your heart and intuition. They somehow already know what you truly want to become. Everything else is secondary."

Having passion for your work also applies to establishing your own business. Don't start a company unless it's an obsession and something you love. If you have an exit strategy, it's not an obsession.

If you don't sacrifice for what you want, what you want will become the sacrifice.

16.

In the soil of a quick fix is often the seed of a new problem.

●

There are no discounts on the price of success.

We all want to get "there" faster, hoping to take a more direct route in reaching the finish line of success ahead of the rest. Most times success is a road you have to travel. When things don't happen right away, just remember: it takes six months to build a Rolls Royce and 13 hours to build a Toyota.

Colonel Harland Sanders first started cooking chicken in his roadside stand in 1930, when he was 40 years old. During the next decade, he worked on his "Secret Recipe" and cooking method for his famous fried chicken, which he sold from various locations. However, in the 1950s, the interstate highway came through the Kentucky town and diverted road traffic from the Colonel's restaurant. He closed his business and retired, disappointed that he hadn't been successful with the fried chicken recipe. But he wasn't done yet. Sanders began asking restaurants to franchise his chicken recipe. Many turned him down before he finally found his first partner and began building his fried chicken empire.

There are two kinds of shortcuts. The first is where you use your knowledge, experience, and intuition to achieve the goal quicker than your competitors. You're working smarter and more creatively to give yourself a competitive edge in order to obtain a more immediate solution. There is usually nothing wrong with that.

Of course, you have to be careful that you're not ignoring an important learning experience or other critical step that may be fundamental to your success. My biggest early career shortcut backfired. I inadvertently bypassed key training that would have ensured my success. My impatience led me to take a shortcut that hindered my overall development and caused more harm than good.

I quickly found there was no elevator to success— I would have to take the stairs.

I've since learned to become a more deliberate, smarter shortcut taker. **I know when to avoid unnecessary delays**, but also not to push the boundaries so far that I miss a valuable lesson or other experience.

My parents always told me that I had to go to college and that was one of my early goals. It's generally accepted that graduates earn substantially more than those who don't finish. However, many highly successful people have taken a shortcut by dropping out of college to launch their careers. Some have found that the impatience to achieve success makes sense. They believe that while formal education will make you a living, self-education may make you a fortune. For example, tech pioneers Bill Gates, Paul Allen, and Michael Dell are among those who determined that a college degree wasn't an absolute necessity.

The second type of shortcut can have dire consequences. If you overlook industry or company regulations, or ignore your own ethical compass, you will be taking a shortcut that endangers you professionally and personally. You may be tempted to engage in unethical practices or even worse—illegal activity. There may be gray areas that are open to interpretation, but most situations are clearly black and white. I am required to protect both myself and those I employ by using the best possible judgment at all times. From a corporate perspective, we make sure that every action is taken with the company's long-term success and security in mind. **No shortcut can ignore industry and professional standards.**

During the country's previous financial crisis and mortgage industry meltdown, I heard the story of a loan officer who was imprisoned because of the fraud he committed with several partners. He tried to explain how he made the transition from a respected mortgage banker to a convict who lost his job, license, and the respect of his family and peers. The disgraced banker insisted that it wasn't his initial intention to break the law; he was only doing what so many others already had—making extra money through some minor paperwork shortcuts. But then he got "caught up" in more serious infractions—a series of illegally obtained loans that benefitted him and his partners. He claimed that, "In the beginning, it was a gray area. I didn't plan on it leading to everything else." Of course, his shortcuts were more than "gray area" detours.

If in doubt, ask yourself whether taking the shortcut is likely to create unnecessary difficulties without the appropriate benefits—either next week or next year.

You'll never regret making a choice based upon doing the right thing.

139

Remember, Coca-Cola only sold 25 bottles its first year. Keep going.

Lunch is
for losers.

17.

Life has no remote. Get up and change it yourself.

•

Stop wasting time. Put down the remote and get off the couch. Stay productive.

You've got to stay engaged and active; otherwise you can easily lose momentum in your daily routine.

I didn't always take that wise advice. Early in my career, when faced with a slow period after finishing a project, I'd often tell myself, "I can finish the other work later. I'll go home early. Tomorrow I'll still be able to meet the deadline." Of course, I missed so many learning and growing opportunities to gain insights into something new and expand my production. One of Wayne Gretzky's favorite sayings is, "You miss 100% of the shots you don't take." Doing your absolute best includes maximizing your greatest resource: time. You'll never plow a field just turning it over in your mind. I gradually developed an attitude that I would do everything possible to stay busy and productive.

You'll never plow a field just turning it over in your mind.

Early in Gold Star's history I was the beneficiary of a powerful lesson that reinforced the importance of remaining productive. When the company was formed, we only had one other loan officer. One day he took a long lunch break, during which time we received several calls from interested homebuyers. I answered the calls and gained three new customers in an hour. I then reminded my colleague that because I was available, I obtained new clients that most likely would have been his. From that point on I have had a "lunch is for losers" attitude. I usually work through lunch; clients know that I am always available. You must understand that there is a direct relationship between the number and length of your non-productive lunches and other breaks and your production and ultimate success. The three new customers I received that day have not only utilized my services numerous times throughout

144

the years, but have also referred many friends and family members. **The next time you're tempted to procrastinate, think about the dividend** I realized from sacrificing one lunch hour.

After Russia was eliminated in the 2016 World Cup of hockey, I received a call around 10:30 p.m. from a Tampa Bay Lightning player who needed a contract for the upcoming season. By 11:30 p.m. I was in negotiations with Tampa's General Manager Steve Yzerman. By 12:15 a.m. we had negotiated the final terms of the contract. It was a good deal for the team, and most importantly, a great deal for my new client. I was on the plane the next morning to sign the contract. Later I learned that the player had been trying to decide between another agent and me. Had I not been able to take his call that night and reach Steve Yzerman, he would have moved on to the other agent. Not every contract can be finalized in an hour and 45 minutes but this one was. There are no secrets to success. It's the result of hard work and always being available.

Thomas Edison is an ideal example of someone who faced

early challenges but achieved amazing success through his impressive work ethic. When Edison was a boy, a teacher insisted he was lazy and not smart enough to succeed in life. Realizing Edison was actually bored, his mother decided to homeschool her son, and she encouraged his wildly creative nature. Edison would eventually prove that teacher wrong, partially because he kept busy and continued to develop new concepts that resulted in a wide variety of inventions.

At 19, Edison went to work for Western Union and asked for the night shift, which allowed him sufficient time to devote to reading and experimenting. In his lifetime, Edison built a manufacturing company and research laboratory, read an entire library, studied qualitative analysis, conducted endless experiments, and patented 1,100 inventions. The "Wizard of Menlo Park" developed the phonograph, made the typewriter functional, invented motion pictures, and demonstrated the first working incandescent light bulb. Edison was fond of saying

"Opportunity is missed by most people because it is dressed in overalls and looks like work."

There is always something to do. Ask for another assignment, read a few articles, help a colleague with a project, or plan the following day's "to do" list. Obviously that doesn't mean "surfing the web" or texting friends. Being busy and productive are two different things.

Remember that it's easy for managers and fellow workers to notice when you're bored and not especially enthusiastic about your work. That's never a good sign.

Next time you find yourself with a few extra minutes or half hour with nothing to do—make yourself useful or learn something new. **Time is your most precious commodity; spend it wisely.**

147

The only time
you run out of chances
is when you stop taking them.

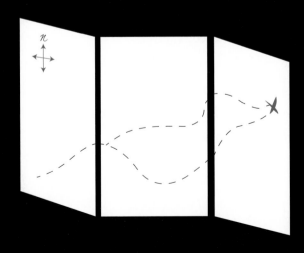

18.

If the plan doesn't work,
change the plan,
NOT the goal.

●

You'll have a better chance of succeeding if you're both stubborn and flexible.

You've got to be adamant about achieving goals and unwilling to compromise on what you consider your most important priorities. However, you also have to be flexible in how you get there. You must adapt to different situations in order to obtain the best results.

Part of being flexible is thinking "outside the box," looking for different options, and being ready to make a change. Henry Ford was definitely a pioneer and "outside-the-box" businessman. Increasing his workers' daily wage was an example of how he strived to be flexible while seeking both productivity and profit.

Anxious to avoid turnover and retain the best workers, Ford knew that he needed to make a change. On January 5, 1914, Ford announced that he would offer qualified workers an increase in their minimum daily pay from $2.34 to $5, more than doubling the rate for most workers. At the time, this was a most unusual move. A

Cleveland, Ohio newspaper, *The Cleveland Plain Dealer,* reported that Ford's announcement "shot like a blinding rocket through the dark clouds of the present industrial depression."

Ford's unexpected decision to increase worker pay was profitable indeed. It attracted some of Detroit's best mechanics and other workers. It eliminated constant turnover, minimized training costs, and significantly boosted productivity.

Companies—and people—that don't adapt often get left behind. When announcing that Nokia had been acquired by Microsoft, then Nokia CEO Stephen Elop said, "We didn't do anything wrong, but somehow we lost." He and his management team were obviously upset. It wasn't that Nokia had done any one thing wrong to result in this drastic development. However, the company didn't keep up with the fast-changing business environment. Their competitors were faster and smarter. Nokia didn't adapt.

In the beginning of my sales career, it was obvious there were proven strategies that I should follow to become more productive, but I also looked for creative ways to adapt to new opportunities. I have changed directions—based on economic developments, customer requests, industry trends, and other factors—when I thought it would mean an exceptionally satisfied customer, increased sales, or a more streamlined operational system.

In the beginning of my sales career, it was obvious there were proven strategies that I should follow to become more productive, but I also looked for creative ways to adapt to new opportunities.

As companies become larger, it can be difficult to maintain that flexibility, because "decisions by committee" are often the norm. At Gold Star we have a management structure that includes thorough reviews of major decisions. However, unlike many other organizations, we also don't allow corporate red

FAILURE?

Just another opportunity to
begin more intelligently.

■

tape to prevent us from making quick decisions in those areas that will lead to greater growth and other benefits.

The key is to maintain an open outlook, not holding on to the "one size fits all" or the deadly "we've always done it this way" mentality. It doesn't mean you should ignore your company's or industry's best practices. But typically there is leeway within each area that enables you to make the appropriate modifications that will give you a competitive edge. You just need to recognize those opportunities and be willing to take them.

WHEN THEY SAY
"YOU CAN'T,"
YOU SAY
"WATCH ME!"

19.

I am coming for everything they said I couldn't have.

●

If we stop believing, we stop achieving.

Self-confidence is a critical factor in being successful. Believing in ourselves gives us the confidence to take bold actions.

You must have a positive and confident attitude. When someone asks me, "Have you ever had self-doubts?" I smile and tell them about the long list of reasons I've had to lack confidence. As a teenager I was laughed at because I couldn't speak English . . . wore secondhand clothes . . . lived in a cramped apartment . . . was embarrassed to have to use food stamps. It's a long list. In fact, **I've never really stopped having doubts; I have simply learned to use them as a prime motivator to excel and prove my critics wrong.**

Of course, as I became more successful as a salesman, business owner, speaker, and author, my self-confidence increased. But I've been careful not to think that I "have arrived." Overconfidence can be as big a pitfall as a lack of confidence. I know success is not guaranteed.

I'm only as good as my next customer, my next deal.

As I stressed earlier, **"Success is never owned."** We must pay the rent every day.

It helps to have the support of others who believe in you. Pablo Picasso said that his mother told him, "If you are a soldier, you will become a general. If you are a monk, you will become the Pope." "Instead," Picasso said, "I was a painter and became Picasso."

Self-doubt often occurs when we let others interfere with our goals. We think of the great Meryl Streep as being one of the best actresses ever. But, as a 26-year-old who had yet to make her film debut, Streep found herself in an uncomfortable position when asked by the son of legendary producer Dino De Laurentiis, Sr. to audition for his father's remake of *King Kong*. While the younger De Laurentiis was impressed with Streep's potential, Dino wasn't that enthusiastic. That day while the young actress waited, she

the SKY is not the limit

ONLY YOUR MIND

———————————

heard Dino comment, "che brutta," which Streep knew meant "how ugly." But she didn't let De Laurentiis' harsh words discourage her quest for finding movie roles. Streep has since gone on to win several Academy Awards and an astonishing number of Academy Award nominations. Yet even the most successful people occasionally question their abilities. "I have varying degrees of confidence and self-loathing," Streep said. "You can have a perfectly horrible day where you doubt your talent ... Or think that you're boring and they're going to find out that you don't know what you're doing."

There is a tendency for us to worry about what others think. But remember, people don't have to believe in you. **You have to believe in yourself.** You will not be liked or believed in by everyone. This has nothing to do with achieving your goals.

There are so many people who will tell you that "you can't." When I applied for my first bank job, there were several friends who questioned whether I was capable of succeeding in such a professional environment. But I just smiled and said, "Watch me." You must learn to differentiate between constructive advice that can help you improve and destructive criticism that is aimed at undermining your confidence. Years later, some of those people who didn't think I could make it, and even some of the people who turned me down for jobs, came to me for professional advice.

You also have to wonder about the doubters themselves. Often our most severe critics are those who don't know us and haven't accomplished much. You'll find in life that those who are famous for chronically pointing out shortcomings and flaws in others rarely have very impressive resumes of their own. Critics can usually talk a good game. After all, they've honed their sharp tongues over time, but don't be fooled; they lack substance and good intention.

Never let someone who has done nothing tell you how to do anything.

I NEVER LOSE

Either I win or I learn.

20.

If you are ever having a bad day, just remember that in 1976 Ronald Wayne sold his 10% stake in Apple for $2,300. It's now worth $70 billion.

●

Nobody likes a whiner or a complainer. They are the first cousins of the critic.

Whiners and complainers spread negativity like the flu, which if untreated, can become a serious disease that can damage an individual's and a company's success.

The simple solution is to avoid negativity, and we have to start with ourselves. We all have off days, but if we're stuck in a negative mode for long, an attitude adjustment is warranted.

Feeling sorry for yourself isn't part of the game plan.

If you focus on problems, you will have more problems. If you focus on solutions, you will have more opportunities.

I had sufficient cause to have a negative attitude as a teenager and during some of my early business slumps. But I made a point to

EXCELLENCE is not a skill.

It is an **ATTITUDE.**

remain as upbeat as possible, believing that a "can do" attitude would be a major factor in my long-term success.

Part of contributing to a positive work environment is being supportive of others.

Be an **encourager**;
the world has enough critics already.

It's also important to **stay away from negative people**. They have a problem for every solution. Do whatever you can to avoid spending time with fellow workers or others who are overly negative. They'll drain your energy and hinder your progress. Rather than trying to change the people around you, change the people you choose to be around. You cannot expect to lead a positive life if you surround yourself with negative people.

Tim Tebow has certainly faced negativity on a very public stage. The former Heisman trophy winner and quarterback for several NFL teams was criticized for his playing skills and

169

often mocked for kneeling in prayer on the football field—known as "Tebowing." People also commented on his quoting of biblical phrases and strong belief in abstinence before marriage. But Tebow has worked hard to avoid being adversely affected by a negative atmosphere. "I'll always use the negativity as more motivation to work even harder and become even stronger," he said.

The Gold Star Family of Companies is a fast-paced organization and we ask a lot of our employees, who are also rewarded and recognized appropriately. But we don't tolerate a negative attitude, which if left unchecked can have a serious impact on company culture. When one of our otherwise successful employees seemed to be in a constant negative frame of mind I began paying more attention. It wasn't long before his attitude seemed to affect others around him. We had several conversations about making a change, but unfortunately he wasn't willing to change his outlook. I think he understood when I explained that he wasn't a good fit for our company.

As an agent for athletes, I have seen otherwise talented

players get cut for having a bad attitude. They can be traded or not have their contracts renewed. Bad attitudes are not accepted in sports, or other areas of life.

We all have some control over the amount of negativity we allow into our lives. We just have to force ourselves to make the often hard decisions to avoid the circumstances and people that contribute to it. **Make sure you have only positive, character-driven movers and shakers in your life.**

Money isn't a problem.
A lack of production,
commitment, and
consistant improvement
is your problem.

21.

Hope is not a strategy.

●

If becoming successful means you will have to outmatch and outmaneuver other individuals or companies, you're going to have to find ways to make your competitors step up their game, not the other way around. **If you're going to rise to the top among people with whom you are competing for the same customers or clients, you absolutely must know what your competition is doing.**

One of the most effective ways to get the inside track on your competition is by becoming a Mystery Shopper. Mystery shopping involves calling businesses and consumers to surreptitiously obtain information on how they run every aspect of their organization. If you're not mystery shopping, you are missing a valuable strategy your competition may be using— and one powerful enough to set you apart in the marketplace.

Most salespeople and many companies are fond of claiming they have the best service or the best product. There's an arrogant complacency in thinking your customer will simply believe you're the best because you've said so. You should never be lured into a false sense of security by becoming smug or overconfident. After all, we can't *all* be the best. **Only one company or individual can rightfully claim to be #1.** You'll have no way of knowing for sure how you compare to your competition unless you gain a firsthand knowledge of exactly what they're doing.

Without the "intel" gained from mystery shopping, you'll never know where you truly stand, or what you need to improve.

You can't perfect your strategy or game-plan without first infiltrating their camp and looking at their playbook.

Every one of your competitors knows something you don't.

Your mission is to find out what that is, then learn from and capitalize on that knowledge.

I first experienced mystery shopping as a McDonald's Management Trainee. One of our tasks was to visit various outlets, posing as a customer, and see how the staff handled their drive-thru and walk-in responsibilities. We were charged with thoroughly evaluating attitude and other communication, teamwork, food prep, cleanliness, service, and everything in-between. It was an exhaustive assessment and an incredible learning experience. I found out early on that you can't do today's job with yesterday's methods or mediocre service and be in business tomorrow. You must take nothing for granted and continually improve.

Years later I realized I could employ the valuable process of mystery shopping within the fiercely competitive arenas of banking and sports management. I not only learn about my rivals' specific strategies and offerings but also study how they present themselves and their companies—whether they seem enthusiastic or bored, upbeat or negative, and how and why they come across as sincere and credible.

My sales call to conversion rate is 78.5 percent. This means that I *do not lose* 78.5 percent of my prospects once we've had an initial contact—whether it's in person or by phone. Compare this with the average sales conversion rate which is right around three percent. I'm able to gain 75% more customers than my average competitor. Why the difference? Because I *know* my enemy.

Every Friday I pick up the phone to mystery shop my competition in order to find out exactly what they are doing and saying and how they're doing and saying it. My goal is always to be better than I was yesterday, and I guarantee by Friday afternoon, I'm better than I was on Thursday. I pay particular attention to how my competition responds to difficult questions and how my objections are addressed. I listen to how respectfully they treat their potential customers and what they say about *my* company when I casually mention our name as a potential service provider. Most other salespeople don't mystery shop consistently enough; you'll need to do it religiously. You'll want to identify the "best of the best" strategies, pitches and presentation techniques. Then take it up a notch.

179

You need to work until your idols become your rivals.

If you're inclined to discount this chapter by deluding yourself into thinking you have no competitors—no "enemy"—know that *everyone* can benefit from mystery shopping as we're always competing at every stage of life. For example, it's an especially valuable tool when you're applying for a job, competing for a promotion, or starting a company. You need to know what you're up against in terms of other candidates or area businesses with whom you're about to step in the ring. You need to sell against and around their strong points. You'll feel more confident and be a far more impressive candidate or business owner if you can demonstrate topic or market intelligence beyond the norm. Mystery shopping can be adapted to any situation where going the extra mile to gain inside information will give you a competitive edge. Success or failure is only determined by where you decide to stop. Remember, amateurs practice until they get it right. **Professionals practice until they can't get it wrong.**

I've observed two reasons why people don't mystery shop. They're either uncomfortable with personally conducting the research, or they're just plain lazy. The first excuse can be eliminated with a little planning and practice. The "acting" aspect of mystery shopping may be out of your comfort zone, but you don't have the luxury of allowing your perceived limitations to diminish your potential advantages. Courage and adaptability must become your day-to-day habits or you'll quickly fall behind. If apathy or laziness is stopping you, I'm wondering why you don't deserve your best. Invest in yourself.

Trust me, you can't afford not to.

Formal education will make you a living; self-education will make you a fortune. Life wants you to win, but you must get out of your own way.

WINNERS

are not the people who never fail,

but the people who **never quit.**

22.

Don't be afraid to fail.

Be afraid to not try.

●

Fear can be both a motivating force and an obstacle to success.

Smart people know that having a reasonable "fear" in certain situations can be advantageous. They are more aware of what to expect and able to anticipate the red flags of potential obstacles—and this gives them an edge in planning and execution. Without that more cautious approach, it's easy to become overconfident and make careless mistakes.

However, if not dealt with appropriately, fear can be paralyzing and keep you from succeeding at work or in other areas of your life. The challenge is to separate your "legitimate," manageable fears—whether it's speaking in public, interviewing for a job, or handling a difficult leadership role—from more irrational phobias such as a fear of sharks or excessive heights, which are unlikely to impact your everyday life.

Analyze the specific situation and **force yourself** to break the uncomfortable activity into more manageable steps— or **"just deal with it."**

A fear of speaking in large gatherings has been a problem for many people, including Harrison Ford, Winston Churchill and Tiger Woods. As highlighted in the movie *The King's Speech*, the Duke of York suddenly became King George VI in 1937 when his brother abdicated the throne to marry a commoner. But King George VI had a severe stuttering problem that made speaking in public extremely difficult. The king found a therapist who gradually taught him how to deal with his fear of speaking so that he could make many radio broadcasts and public presentations throughout World War II and after.

You must **identify and utilize every available resource** to build upon your strengths and correct

NO MATTER HOW YOU FEEL,

get up,

dress up,

show up,

and never give up.

weaknesses. Take the necessary steps to enhance your "marketability." That's also part of your job.

Professional athletes face enough challenges without having to endure deafness. But Curtis Pride, who became deaf shortly after birth, was determined to "play ball." He was a three-sport star in high school and upon graduation entered the minor league baseball system. In 1993, he was admitted to "the show" with the Montreal Expos, and was a major leaguer for 11 years.

Some people simply fear the "unknown"—trying something different and possibly failing. They often anticipate that situations will be of greater concern than they actually are, and worry needlessly about the "what ifs." Stop being afraid of what could go wrong and **focus on what could go right**. Don't obsess about future problems.

There's also no reason to unnecessarily call attention to your fears. I've heard that some of our employees have commented that I appear to be "fearless," rarely demonstrating worry over major issues. That's most likely because I generally appear calm in difficult situations, not wanting to seem especially vulnerable to competitors and others. But being "fearless" is not entirely accurate. I have concerns that sometimes keep me up at night: shifts in the economy, our country, and the welfare of Gold Star employees. However, I have learned to concentrate on the areas over which I have some control, and try to ignore the many external events that will occur whether or not I worry about them.

Ultimately you have to figure out a way to control your fears so that they don't control you and become an unmovable obstacle.

Positive thinking breeds courageous habits.

If you're constantly fighting your fears, you'll always be trapped on the defensive side of a battle. Instead, face your fears and you'll be free forever.

Being challenged in life is inevitable; being defeated is optional.

23.

FAILURE IS THE BEST TEACHER

Never a failure.
Always a lesson.

●

In order to succeed you must be willing to fail.

Obviously you don't begin a job, assignment, or anything else thinking that failing is acceptable. Your goal should always be to approach every job or relationship as if it will be successful. If you begin something with the overriding thought that you could fail, you may not do your best. Or worse, you may never begin. Your biggest risk will be the one you don't take.

However, failures are inevitable, especially when you take a big risk to achieve ambitious goals. Michael Dell said, "Recognize that there will be failures and acknowledge that there will be obstacles. But you will learn from your mistakes and the mistakes of others, for there is very little learning in success."

Failure is not falling down but refusing to get up. Most successful people have failed on their way to achieving their goals, but their

EXCUSES
are thieves...
THEY STEAL
your dreams.

resilient nature and dogged determination to succeed sets them apart from the quitters. Vince Lombardi, considered one of the greatest coaches and motivators in NFL history, said, "Remember, the man on top of the mountain didn't fall there." People who reach the top aren't afraid of the climb.

Henry Ford's early businesses failed and left him broke five times before he founded Ford Motor Company; Steve Jobs was fired by his own board; Michael Jordan didn't make the roster on his school basketball team; and earlier in his life Abraham Lincoln had numerous business failures, lost seven elections, and barely got 100 votes in his quest for the vice presidential nomination, before finally being elected as the sixteenth President of the United States.

Failures are usually only temporary.

Walt Disney is recognized for his creativity and many successes. But he also had his share of failures. Disney's film *Bambi* didn't recover its production expenses and was considered a financial failure at the time. However, it received three Academy Award nominations and subsequent releases after World War II, which helped make the film one of the industry's major financial successes.

Jack Ma, the creator of Alibaba Group, a family of successful internet-based businesses, is the world's 22nd richest man, but he hasn't always considered himself a success. He failed three times in college. Ma applied 30 times to get a job but was always rejected. When Kentucky Fried Chicken was introduced to China, he and 23 other people sought employment; he was the only one dismissed. He applied ten times to Harvard, but was rejected. Ma obviously learned from the failures and rejections. *Forbes* has reported his net worth to be more than $30 billion.

I stumbled myself a couple of times. My own failures came after several successful years in the consumer lending profession. I was so confident of my abilities and past accomplishments that I was sure I could succeed as a mortgage broker. It didn't take long for me to realize that I wasn't sufficiently prepared, and I met the wake-up call of failure.

Like many others who persevere in the face of disappointment, I chose to learn from those failures and move on. I was fortunate to learn an early lesson—that your best teacher is your last mistake. With that mindset I refused to allow failure to slow my momentum or derail my dream. Failure is a great tool we can use to chart a better course and refine strategy; it's an opportunity to begin more intelligently.

Failure isn't losing; it's learning.

People are often so afraid they'll fail at something that they don't give a full effort. Don't be afraid to fail, be afraid not to try. Michael Jordan said, "I can accept failure. Everyone has failed. But I can't accept not trying." Being challenged in life is inevitable; being defeated is optional.

197

OPPORTUNITIES

are usually disguised
as impossible situations.

24.

Most people don't see an opportunity until it doesn't exist anymore. Don't be most people!

●

ABC—"Always Be Closing"—is one of my favorite phrases, a motto that I live by and one of the main reasons for my many successes.

It emphasizes the importance of being in a constant "moving forward" mode.

You should never turn off your selling mindset. Always be ready to engage a friend, colleague, or stranger in conversations that could lead to a sale or opportunity. I am especially interested in pursuing unexpected sales opportunities, the type that some overlook and the more enterprising salespeople embrace. I have met some of the best sales prospects at fundraising dinners and sporting events, on airplanes, and even on vacation. I'm always observing, selling and closing.

You must be aware of the ABC opportunities.

A police officer stopped a Gold Star loan originator who was speeding on his way to an evening client meeting. The policeman seemed to be interested that our employee was a mortgage loan officer. After exchanging his business card for the speeding ticket, our originator drove a little slower to his customer meeting. The next morning he received a phone call from the policeman who was looking for a good deal on his new loan.

ABC applies to everyone—because we are all salespeople.

If you're not selling a product or service, you are selling yourself or your ideas—

to a manager, a potential employer, or a professional organization. "Closing" doesn't just refer to completing the sale; **it means being open to and seizing new growth opportunities—**whether that means more business, a new job, career advancement, or personal

SUCCESS

doesn't happen to you.

It happens

BECAUSE

of you.

development. It also means continuing to learn, stretching your limits, testing new ideas and always moving forward.

Joy Mangano was a divorced mother of three who could barely afford to pay the bills. She had always had great ideas, and one day, decided to give up the menial jobs she had been holding to chase her dream. She wanted to try to market her invention of a self-wringing mop. In order to do this, she had to sell her idea to an investor and to potential customers. Ultimately, she got a chance to show it to a buyer at the QVC shopping channel. When the mop failed to sell on QVC with an actor, Mangano convinced the buyer to let her go on live television and sell her product herself. The results were phenomenal, and her invention, known as the Miracle Mop, ended up grossing $10 million a year. She went on to create her company, Ingenious Designs, and her inventions made her a multi-millionaire. If Mangano hadn't kept selling her product and had given up, she would have never grown the empire she has today.

Savvy businesspeople and others take advantage of the many ABC scenarios: occasions when they interact with potential new customers or other important contacts. However, I've seen many others who are lazy, and not willing to take the time to learn and profit from these encounters. Those who stop paying attention "after hours" or otherwise miss signals that could lead to future sales and other benefits are not demonstrating the commitment and passion required to excel.

If you're not receptive to the basic ABC principles, you'll never reach your full potential. You can't expect extraordinary results from average work. You'll join the mediocre majority, letting great success slip through your fingers.

Opportunity only presents itself when you **present yourself**.

You are not a product of
your circumstances.
You are a product
of your decisions.

25.

Nobody is taller than the last man standing.

●

Don't be a "survivor," someone who merely "gets by."

Surviving means that you will settle for "hanging on."

Of course, there are many situations where surviving itself is an accomplishment, such as making it through a health challenge or some type of emergency. But I'm talking about the many other challenges we all face.

During America's financial crisis that was precipitated by the major subprime mortgage disaster, many lenders and other financial institutions were treading water, trying to hang on and not close their doors or be faced with mass downsizing. It was a desperate situation. I watched companies and banks shutting down all around us, the recession claiming 62% of our competition. Even though my company faced the same basic challenges, I was determined that Gold Star would do more than just "survive" this. We would not be buried in the rubble of defeat.

I called a company-wide meeting and, looking at the sagging shoulders and somber expressions of my people, I realized I was about to give the most important speech of my career. I announced in a clear, strong voice that Gold Star would NOT be participating in the world's recession. I went on to assure them that although many of their spouses and family members had lost jobs, theirs would be secure with Gold Star. **I vowed that we would emerge from these trying times stronger than ever—**and explained how we were going to capitalize on the recession as the platform for our growth strategy.

The mood in the room changed, and from that day forward, we put the pedal to the metal, remained upbeat, and never looked back. That year, because of our collective conviction, we opened a number of branches, recruited the industry's top talent, and significantly expanded our national footprint, growing by over 700%. This expansion led to us being named among *Inc.* 500's fastest-growing companies in the United

States. The growth was sustainable. Our business doubled the following year.

For several uncomfortable years, British author J.K. Rowling was in "survivor" mode. In 1994, three years before *Harry Potter and The Philosopher's Stone* was published, Rowling had recently divorced and was raising a young child on her own while receiving government aid. Because she was unable to afford a computer or the cost of copying her now famous manuscript, Rowling had to manually type each version for publishers.

But Rowling had the spirit and determination of someone who wasn't content to "settle." Despite a difficult situation, the fledgling author continued to believe in herself and the story she had created. After many rejections, a small London publisher finally took a chance and published *Harry Potter and The Philosopher's Stone*, which was the first in a highly successful series of books and movies, providing Rowling with worldwide acclaim. She is now one of the United Kingdom's wealthiest citizens.

In order to thrive—both professionally and personally— you have to shift your mindset from a surviving to thriving mode.

Being a successful "thriver" involves having an effective plan, working hard, looking for special opportunities to excel, raising the bar, and maintaining a positive attitude no matter what.

The key is to develop the "thrive" attitude in advance so that you're prepared when dealing with a potentially overwhelming situation where you might ordinarily be content to "merely" survive. You are not a product of your circumstances. You are a product of your decisions. You will distinguish yourself at the top if you become a habitual "thriver."

section

Turn Your Ideas
Into Action

Twenty years from now you'll be more disappointed by the things you didn't do than by the ones you did.

—MARK TWAIN

All of the well-known success stories highlighted in this book have something critically important in common. ***These people took action.*** They found their passion, formulated ambitious goals, ignored harsh critics, learned from failure . . . and acted decisively. They acted boldly in their relentless pursuit of the dreams others said were far beyond their grasp, and didn't allow anything to stand in their way.

Success saboteurs of self-doubt, physical challenge, fear and adversity were no match for their determination. So many of the core values I've shared with you—those values I've frequently referred to as life-changing—appear throughout the legendary success stories of these fearless "thrivers."

Winners are not the people who never fail; they are the people who never quit.

Many people wish to improve their personal or professional lives so they read a book, attend a lecture, listen to a motivational program, or work with a personal coach. They usually learn valuable insights and proven strategies for improvement and achieving greater success. Initially, they are excited about the information they've received. They leave the conference hall with an extra measure of enthusiasm, fired up by imagining the potential rewards that seem within their grasp. But too many quickly slip back to their previous comfort-zone routine, neglecting to initiate any of the lessons that could help move them forward. The motivational flame flickers and dies before they act.

Certainly some people who read this book are already quite successful. They're at or near the top of the mountain and will do everything in their power to stay there. They are continually growing, and will use my experiences, as well as suggestions from others, as additional resources to enhance their master plan. Others have decided to make a change and begun to map out their course of action, evaluating the success concepts they feel will be most effective.

Many will remain stuck in the quicksand of procrastination, rationalizing that it isn't possible to get started. If you are in that unfortunate position, **it's time to deal with the self-saboteurs that are robbing you of the life you deserve.**

Albert Einstein said, "I am thankful for all of those who said NO to me. It's because of them I am doing it myself."

If you've not yet taken the time to chart a course for your dreams, you must begin this process now. It will be the most important reality check you'll ever make. I challenge you to take the next two or three available hours to determine what you want to achieve. Take your laptop or pen and paper and do the soul-searching required to put a finer point on your highest aspirations. Don't write through a filter of perceived limitations; boldly state the future you envision.

Outline your basic plan and list how you will reach those ambitious goals and dreams. You don't have to detail every step—just the main elements. Write down what **specific actions** are required for you to get from your current situation to your desired new place. Don't forget the timetable; you must **establish some deadlines** to meet the various stages of your end goals.

220

Be willing to make some major adjustments; you won't get "there" without a few sacrifices.

This will be the foundation upon which you'll build the next phase of your life—for the next day, the next week, the next year, and beyond. The best way to predict the future is to create it.

If you're sabotaging your success by telling yourself that life has passed you by, or that you don't have enough time left to truly make your mark, you may want to spend a little time familiarizing yourself with Ray Kroc, who in his lifetime worked his uncle's soda fountain, sold everything from lemonade and paper cups to real estate, ran a radio station, drove an ambulance, and was 52 years old and in poor health the day he drove to California to find out why a little burger joint would need five of the milkshake Multi-Mixers he was selling at the time. What he found were two brothers, Richard and Maurice McDonald, whose restaurant was a smash hit with the locals.

221

People couldn't get enough of the "quickly prepared," inexpensive burgers, fries and shakes and flocked from ten counties to eat there. As Ray watched the line of cars wrap around the parking lot and cause a traffic jam in the street, he smiled and imagined hundreds of these restaurants causing traffic jams all over the country. Ray Kroc launched his dream at a time when most people are thinking of retiring. He became the McDonald brothers' managing partner, and turned their restaurant into the world's most successful restaurant chain.

We all have the ability to leap at greater opportunity and to change in order to succeed, but hope is not a strategy. You must be ready to choose a direction and move forward. I promise you will never regret taking the first step on your journey toward greater success, as the biggest opportunities of your life are often just inches on the other side of inaction and discouragement. Don't downgrade your dream to fit your reality.

Upgrade your conviction to match your destiny.

You and you alone hold the keys, tools and passion you'll need to create your own success. Everything you need to become #1 lies within you. I certainly don't mean to imply it will be easy. In fact, I guarantee it won't be easy. I do, however, promise you it will be *worth it*.

223

It's never too late to become
what you might have been.

Rising to #1

NEVER GIVE IN. NEVER GIVE UP.

Every mountaintop is within your reach if you just keep climbing.

●

Sometimes people with the worst past end up creating the best future. If things "haven't worked out so far," and you think it's too late for you to reach the top, think again.

Jan Koum's early life definitely didn't indicate that he would eventually become the highly successful creator of one of the most popular phone apps ever produced.

Born and raised in a small village outside of Kiev, Ukraine, he and his parents lived in a house with no hot water. It wasn't an easy life. Like myself, at age 16, Koum and his mother emigrated to America.

Koum and his mother lived off food stamps in the housing projects in Northern California. While he wasn't an exceptional high school student, Koum did look for other opportunities to excel, teaching himself computer networking and other technical skills.

Koum developed the concept for WhatsApp as a free messaging/texting service, which he continued to refine during the next several years. There were many frustrating periods when it wasn't working the way he had expected. At one point he even considered giving up and finding a job. However, by 2011 WhatsApp was considered one of the top 20 apps, and two years later, there were more than 200 million users.

In 2014, Koum decided to sell WhatsApp to Facebook for $19 billion—closing the deal in the building adjacent to the social services office where he once collected food stamps.

Of course, there are many others who have risen above significant obstacles and been extremely successful.

AOL paid Arianna Huffington $315 million for *The Huffington Post*, which she co-founded. However, she has faced a few difficult periods as well. Thirty-six publishers rejected her second book, and *The Huffington Post* initially received some very negative reviews. "I failed many times in my life," she once said. "But my mother used to tell me, **'Failure is not the**

228

opposite of success; it's a steppingstone to success.' So at some point, I learned not to dread failure."

As a youth, Winston Churchill struggled in school and didn't seem destined to be a world leader. He later faced a number of political failures, but then at the age of 62, he was elected prime minister of the United Kingdom—serving his country during World War II. Churchill also won the Nobel Prize.

While Jackie Robinson was the first African American to play Major League Baseball, Larry Doby faced his own huge challenge. As the first African American player in the American League, Doby was taunted, and even ostracized by some of his teammates. But Doby was also able to endure the difficulties, and eventually was elected to the Baseball Hall of Fame.

During his lifetime, Vincent Van Gogh sold only one painting, and this was to a friend for a very small amount of money. While Van Gogh was never a success during his own lifetime, he completed more than 800 known paintings, many of them among the most treasured artwork in the world.

After playing baseball irregularly for the Minnesota Twins for a few years in the 1980s, Jim Eisenreich retired because he was battling with Tourette syndrome. Eisenreich sought treatment and returned to baseball for another decade. He even helped lead the Florida Marlins to the World Series in 1997. Eisenreich was the first recipient of the Tony Conigliaro Award, given to a player who overcomes a major obstacle.

In 1954, Elvis was unknown and not especially respected as a singer. The manager of the Grand Ole Opry even fired him after just one performance, advising that "You ain't going nowhere, son. You ought to go back to driving a truck." Of course, Elvis didn't return to driving, but instead kept singing, receiving worldwide recognition as a singer—the King of Rock and Roll—and a movie star.

An Olympic track star, Louis Zamperini was on a mission to locate missing airmen during World War II when his plane crashed into the ocean. He survived 47 days in a life raft, only to be captured by the Japanese and sent to a labor camp. For the next two years, he endured incredible cruelty at the hands of his ruthless guards and at times thought he wouldn't survive. But toward the end of the war, Zamperini was rescued, and he eventually forgave his captors. For the rest of his life he was a youth camp leader and popular inspirational speaker. His favorite phrase was "Don't give up. Don't give in."

These are only some examples of people who have become successful, despite the odds, or perhaps, because of them. No one is born successful. Success or failure is only determined by where you stop.

Remember
Rule #1: Don't be #2.

—Dan Milstein

acknowledgments

Writing *Rule #1: Don't Be #2* has been an especially rewarding experience—an opportunity to share the values and strategies that have been integral to my success.

Of course, writing a book is a collaborative process and I have benefitted from the support I've received from numerous people.

I'm so fortunate to have such supportive parents who led by courageous example and taught me invaluable lessons. Their early influence helped shape my philosophy of hard work, determination, and never giving up.

I would like to thank everyone at the Gold Star Family of Companies for their ongoing commitment to consistently raising the bar in order to meet and surpass personal and corporate goals.

I am particularly grateful to those who were instrumental in the development and production of this book. David Robinson's editorial skills and creativity were key in developing the concept and content, similar to two of my earlier books. It has been a very enjoyable and productive association.

Special thanks to Pamela Gossiaux for her valuable editing support and to Cheryl Baringer who assisted with several key sections.

Scott Lorenz has once again provided his publishing and promotional expertise, and has also been a reliable sounding board for everything from book titles to marketing plans.

I am also deeply appreciative to the many who have shared their own stories of rising above difficult challenges and daunting failures to achieve personal and professional success. You have truly inspired me.

I am indebted to everyone who helped make this book a reality.

about the author

DANIEL MILSTEIN is the Founder and CEO of the Gold Star Family of Companies, operating in over 40 offices worldwide, specializing in financial services, sports management, publishing and film production. Under Dan's visionary leadership, Gold Star has been named among *Inc.* magazine's 500 Fastest Growing Companies in America.

Dan was born in the Soviet Union and was just 16 when he narrowly escaped the turbulent aftermath of the Chernobyl Disaster, emigrating to the United States in 1991 in search of a better life. Arriving with only 17 cents in his pocket, but fueled by his determination to seize the American Dream, Dan first hurdled the challenges of immigration, then stormed every opportunity in his path, quickly rising to the rank of #1 Loan Officer in the country out of 550,000 lending industry professionals.

Dan's ability to consistently maintain record-breaking sales, while simultaneously developing sustainable corporations and establishing an international advisory presence among the world's top athletes, has routinely landed him on America's most notable lists of the youngest and most impressive entrepreneurs. He's been included in the prestigious "40 Under 40" in *Crain's* magazine, "30 in Their Thirties" by *dBusiness* magazine and numerous rosters of Top Finance Professionals.

Demonstrating a decades-long ability to maximize opportunity for himself and others, Dan's passion for mentoring led to the expansion and diversification of Gold Star and launched his writing career in 2010. Now the award-winning, international best-selling author of *The ABC of Sales, 17 Cents and a Dream* and *Street Smart Selling,* Dan adds the greatly anticipated *Rule #1: Don't Be #2* to his body of work. Consultant, speaker and member of the esteemed National Academy of Best-Selling Authors, Milstein is credited with motivating hundreds of thousands with his simple, yet powerful, brand of inspiration.